MATCHA COOKBOOK

55 MATCHA RECIPES FOR ENERGY, HEALTH & LONGEVITY

K. HELMSTETTER

ABOUT THE AUTHOR

Kristen Helmstetter is an author traveling the world with her family on a multi-year odyssey to experience other cultures and stay fit while she stuffs her face with their food. (For now, meat anyway.)

See Kristen's blog at:

HappySexyMillionaire.me

Twitter: @KristensRaw

Instagram: Kristen_Helmstetter

Copyright © 2018 Kristen Suzanne Helmstetter

All rights reserved. No part of this book shall be reproduced, stored in a retrieval system, or transmitted by any means, electronic, mechanical, photocopying, recording, or otherwise, without written permission from the publisher. Although every precaution has been taken in the preparation of this book, the publisher and author assume no responsibility for errors or omissions. Nor is any liability assumed for damages resulting from the use of the information contained herein.

For information on excerpting, reprinting or licensing portions of this book, please write to info@greenbutterflypress.com.

CONTENTS

Also by K. Helmstetter — vii
Introduction — ix

PART I
BEVERAGES

Licorice Root Matcha Tea	2
1-Minute Matcha Vanilla Pumpkin Seed Milk	4
Fresh Minted Spicy Hot Matcha Latte	5
Matcha Pumpkin Spice Tea	6
Creamy Iced Indian Spiced Matcha Latte	7
Cold Coffee-Matcha Power	8
Matcha Bone Broth	10
Matcha Green Buddha Beer	11
Iced Collagen Matcha	12
Spicy Matcha Metabolism Booster	13
A "Healthy" Matcha Green Smoothie	14
Tropical Turmeric Matcha Smoothie	16
Chocolate Matcha Workout Shake	17
Iced Lime Matcha Refresher	18
Coconut Water Yoga Matcha	19
Matcha Vanilla Butter Latte	20
Zen Tonic Herb Matcha	21
Creamy Coconut Matcha	22
Bulletproof™ Matcha Vanilla Butter Latte	23
Grapefruit Matcha Chia Fresca	24
Meditation Matcha	25
Warming Magical Matcha Elixir	26
Sparkling Matcha Water	27
Rose Petal Matcha Romance Tea	28
Matcha Cinnamon Blend	29
Umeboshi Ginger Matcha Digestion Tea	30

PART II
FOOD

Matcha Buttered Organic Popcorn	32
Lucky Matcha Mashed Potatoes	34
Lady Bugs on a Mossy Log	35
Matcha Grass-Fed Butter Spread	37
Matcha Mini Pesto	38
Matcha Spicy Tahini Dressing (or Dip)	40
Sweet Lemon Matcha Salad Dressing	41
Maple Matcha Gummies	43
Matcha Breakfast Energy Yogurt	44
Softly Scrambled Matcha Eggs	45
Matcha Cardamom Gluten-Free Blender Pancakes	47
Apple Pear Matcha "Porridge"	49
Matcha Banana Mash	50
Matcha Whipped Cream	52
Matcha Energy Nut Butter	53
Matcha-Dusted, Garlic-Buttered Mochi	55
Matcha Guacamole	56
Matcha Tuna Salad	58
Matcha Ice Cubes	60
Almond Allspice Matcha Chia Pudding	62
Lemon Matcha Chocolate Pudding	63
Matcha Breakfast Coconut Ice Cream (Low-Carb)	64
Sweet Matcha Bars	66
Simple Broccoli Matcha Soup	69
Chilled Matcha Beauty Soup	70
Matcha Miso Soup	71
Coconut Mint Chip Matcha Ice Cream	72

PART III
FACIAL MASKS

Matcha Beauty Mask	74
Matcha 'n' Aloe Healing Skin Mask	76

Conclusion   77

ALSO BY K. HELMSTETTER

Coffee Self-Talk

5 Minutes a Day to Start Living Your Magical Life

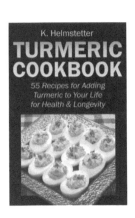

Turmeric Cookbook

55 Recipes for Adding Turmeric to Your Life for Health & Longevity

K. SUZANNE'S ROMANCE NOVELS

Under the pen name, Brisa Starr

Lockdown Love

His Secret

Save Me

Sweet as Pie

Fake It (September 2020)

INTRODUCTION

When I set out to make this book it was simply because of my passion for matcha: the flavor, the experience, the health benefits. I instantly saw how I could use matcha in many ways from drinks to dressings to desserts and more, and that's what you have in this book -- plenty of recipes for matcha to make an appearance in your life, too.

If you're not very familiar with matcha, let me introduce you. Matcha tea, a nutritious Japanese tea ceremony beverage, is basically green tea. But, it's much more... it's like green tea on steroids. The difference between matcha and other green tea is that, with matcha tea, the leaves are ground and consumed "whole" instead of steeped, which makes for a powerful drink for both mind and body. It's filled with nutrition, including antioxidants, chlorophyll, vitamins, and it can help your body in a number of ways.

I'm drawn to matcha for three main reasons:

1. Meditation and Alpha Brain Waves for Feeling Truly Great

Our brains produce different brainwaves, based on our mood and state-of-mind throughout the day. These waves can be measured using an EEG machine. Alpha waves are important because they're the brain waves that help you flow through life with less stress and agitation.

We can experience a deep sense of relaxation and wellness when our brains are producing alpha brain waves.

Alpha brain waves are also associated with creativity, which is why artists and many entrepreneurs are found to exhibit alpha brain waves when they're doing their best work.

There are a few ways to increase your alpha brain waves: meditation, yoga, and—guess what?—drinking matcha!

Meditation is one way to get more alpha brain waves into your life. In meditation, practitioners strive to reach the alpha brain wave state, but this is usually difficult for those who are new to meditation. You can also generate alpha brain waves while doing yoga, though this is likely because a lot of people enter a meditative frame of mind while practicing yoga.

Green tea has a reputation for making meditation—and the benefits of meditation—more accessible because of the alpha waves green tea creates. Think of it as a hack. As you might imagine, drinking green tea as matcha green tea, meaning the whole leaf is consumed, can amp up these effects big time. Drinking a strong cup of matcha green tea before meditation (or yoga) can jumpstart the state of a calm, Zen energy that primes mind and body for a great session.

2. Energy (or Zenergy)

Matcha is a great way to get a bit of energy that doesn't stress your body out like coffee can. It's a perfect early-afternoon drink to give you just enough energy to finish the day strong. Energy and happiness, that's matcha's gift.

Matcha is known for offering a slower release of energy due to being absorbed more slowly by the body. Dave Asprey of BulletproofExec.com writes, "It contains l-theanine, a relaxing amino acid that smoothes out the stimulating effects of caffeine." L-theanine and caffeine in combination are beneficial for improving performance on cognitively demanding tasks.

Tea is liquid wisdom.

—Anonymous

3. Nutrition

Green tea, especially matcha green tea powder, is an excellent source of antioxidants (more than coffee), notably as the powerful polyphenol, catechins. By drinking green tea as matcha, where the whole leaf is consumed, you get a bigger dose.

These antioxidants are antiviral and anti-inflammatory, so I like to drink extra matcha during cold and flu season or if I'm doing any strenuous exercise. Matcha is also known to have a variety of vitamins and trace minerals, and it's ridiculously impressive on the Oxygen Radical Absorbance Capacity (ORAC) scale, ranking much higher than common superfoods like goji berries, chocolate, acai berries, wild blueberries, and pomegranate.

People drink matcha for massive immune-boosting benefits, anti-aging brain health, digestion support, skin renewal, powerful relaxation effects while attaining mental alertness, joint health, cardiovascular health, metabolism-boosting benefits, detoxification (from the chlorophyll), energy-amping qualities, and for helping prevent and fight cancer. And if that weren't enough, many people claim it helps keep their breath fresh.

Dr. Andrew Weil writes, "Studies either strongly suggest or confirm that the antioxidants in green tea can reduce LDL cholesterol, promote fat burning, reduce the risk of several forms of cancer, and alleviate depression."

Risks of Matcha?

The risks of drinking matcha are few. It does contain caffeine, with some varieties listing 25 to 35 milligrams of caffeine per gram of matcha tea. This is not very much unless you're doubling and tripling the serving. If you're sensitive to caffeine, you might discuss drinking matcha with your physician. It also has been shown to reduce serum folate levels in pregnant women. Therefore, again, discuss drinking matcha with your physician if you're pregnant (or breastfeeding), and find ways to add more folate to your diet with foods such as organic spinach, broccoli, asparagus, and pasture-raised egg yolks.

In my experience, I've also found that matcha on an empty stomach can make me nauseous.

As with many things in life, moderation can be smart. Same goes for consuming matcha.

A Few Things About These Recipes

Gluten

All of my recipes are free of gluten, except for the recipe that calls for beer.

Low Carb

Most of these recipes are also low in carbohydrates, due to the health benefits of avoiding too much sugar. Depending on the source, matcha green tea can be bitter, so if you need more water to dilute it, or if you prefer sweetness, then please feel free to adjust these recipes to taste.

Just Add Matcha!

You'll notice that many of these recipes are common things you'd make in the kitchen, and all I did was add some matcha. That's deliberate, as I'm more interested in helping people add matcha to their diets than I am in making matcha the star of the show. To me, it's an ingredient. An amazing ingredient, to be sure, but still just an ingredient. So many of these recipes involve simply adding matcha to things... because we can. They serve to open your eyes and mind to a new way of thinking about matcha and my hope is that these recipes will inspire you to use matcha in many ways, beyond these recipes, that would not have considered previously.

Temperature

I never expose my matcha to high temperatures. I prefer to use it in recipes that won't cook using high heat because I don't want to harm the nutrients or compromise the flavor.

Special Equipment

You'll see many aficionados consuming matcha from a special matcha bowl. The matcha gets whisked in this bowl with a special bamboo whisk. I think that's great, and lends some ceremonial grooviness, but it's not necessary. The recipes in this book were made using an electric hand whisk or my blender. Sometimes I already had the matcha in a bottle and I simply shook it up with some other liquid. Easy peasy.

Sifting Matcha

When drinking a traditional cup of matcha, people whisk the matcha with the water. As mentioned above, the whisk is either a bamboo whisk, or in my case, an electric frothing whisk available at Amazon.com. In either case, you'll get a smooth beverage without clumps if the matcha is sifted prior to whisking. To do this, I have a fine mesh sifter, which I use to sift a few tablespoons at a time into a dark-colored glass jar for storage (in the refrigerator, for up to a month). That way, I don't have to sift every time I get my matcha urge, and I find that removing this little bit of friction is a great way to make sure matcha is a part of my daily routing. That said, there are many times when I simply use my high-speed blender to do the work, which means I don't need to sift.

Storing Matcha

There are several approaches to storing matcha, with no approach universally agreed upon. Many people recommend keeping your unopened bags in the refrigerator or freezer. Once opened, take some out (maybe a week's worth) and store it in a dark glass jar (also in the refrigerator), while keeping the remaining portion in the refrigerator until you need more. This prevents constantly opening and closing the main source, which will keep it fresher longer. Yet others recommend that, once the package is opened, keep it in a cool dark space, but not the refrigerator. My best rule-of-thumb is to only buy a little at a time and consume it fairly quickly so it doesn't sit around.

Where to Get Matcha

I buy matcha from:

Yuki-cha.com

BreakawayMatcha.com

"I take the act of drinking matcha seriously—or perhaps I should say, I take the pleasure of drinking matcha seriously."

—Dr. Andrew Weil

PART I
BEVERAGES

LICORICE ROOT MATCHA TEA

Yield 1 serving

This is one of my favorites. It's lightly sweet and energizing. Licorice root is reputed to be good for the adrenals, too. However, people with unhealthy blood pressure should check with their doctor before consuming licorice root.

- *3/4 cup water*
- *1 teaspoon licorice root*

- *1/2 teaspoon matcha green tea powder*

In a small pot, bring the water and licorice root to a simmer for two to three minutes. Turn off the stove and let it cool to 175 degrees F.

When the licorice root tea is cool enough, strain the liquid into a cup with the matcha. Froth or whisk to mix.

1-MINUTE MATCHA VANILLA PUMPKIN SEED MILK

Yield 1 serving

A creamy delicious drink to be enjoyed by itself, with a few cookies, or over your next bowl of granola.

- *1 cup water*
- *1 dash vanilla bean powder*
- *2 tablespoons pumpkin seed butter*
- *1 teaspoon matcha green tea powder*
- *1 teaspoon raw honey, optional*

Blend all of the ingredients together until smooth and creamy. Add a spoonful of cacao powder to make it chocolaty.

FRESH MINTED SPICY HOT MATCHA LATTE

Yield 1 serving

Consuming MCT oil combined with cayenne boosts metabolism, thus creating heat. It's called "diet-induced thermogenesis."

- *1 1/4 to 1 1/2 cups hot water, 175 degrees F*
- *2 teaspoons matcha green tea powder*
- *1 to 2 tablespoons grass-fed (unsalted) butter*
- *1 tablespoon MCT oil*
- *6 fresh mint leaves*
- *1/8 to 1/4 teaspoon ground cayenne pepper powder, to taste*
- *4 to 5 drops liquid stevia*

Blend everything until creamy and frothy.

MATCHA PUMPKIN SPICE TEA

Yield 1 serving

This is one of my favorite ways to drink matcha tea. You'll be surprised at how wonderfully these ingredients pair.

- 1/2 cup hot water, 175 degrees F
- 1/2 teaspoon matcha green tea powder, sifted
- 2 pinches pumpkin spice powder

Froth or whisk the ingredients together.

CREAMY ICED INDIAN SPICED MATCHA LATTE

Yield 1 serving

A hint of Indian spices takes this buttered latte to the next level.

- *1 cup hot water, 175 degrees F*
- *3/4 teaspoon matcha green tea powder*
- *1 tablespoon grass-fed (unsalted) butter*
- *3-finger pinch fennel seeds*
- *3-finger pinch ground allspice*
- *1 cup ice*

Blend the hot water with the matcha, butter, fennel seeds, and allspice. Pour over ice and serve.

COLD COFFEE-MATCHA POWER

Yield 1 serving

Some days call for having both coffee and matcha.

- *2 cups freshly brewed organic coffee*
- *1 to 2 teaspoons grated raw cacao butter*
- *1 to 2 tablespoons grass-fed (unsalted) butter*
- *2 tablespoons grass-fed collagen protein powder*
- *ice cubes*
- *1/2 teaspoon matcha green tea powder*

Blend the coffee, cacao butter, dairy butter, and collagen together. Add a few ice cubes to cool it. Blend in the matcha. Serve over ice.

MATCHA BONE BROTH

Yield 1 serving

Bone broth is nutritious and we drink it by the mug often. There are days that I'd love to have bone broth for breakfast, but I couldn't imagine not getting my bump of caffeine energy. Well, that's not a problem with Matcha Bone Broth.

You can buy bone broth/stock (they're the same thing). Or learn to make your own with my Bone Broth book.

- *1 to 2 cups bone broth or stock*
- *1/2 teaspoon matcha green tea powder*
- *sea salt, if needed*

Heat the bone broth to 175 degrees F. Transfer the bone broth to a blender with the matcha. Blend and pour into a mug. Season with sea salt, if needed.

MATCHA GREEN BUDDHA BEER

Yield 1 serving

I don't drink beer, but my husband does and he suggested we add matcha to a beer. Would you believe we even had a random bottle of Lucky Buddha beer in the fridge? Clearly, the universe's way of saying, "Sure, Kristen, add matcha to beer."

- *1 bottle Lucky Buddha beer, or any pilsner style beer*
- *1/8 to 1/4 teaspoon matcha green tea powder, sifted*

Pour about an ounce of beer into a cold glass. Add the sifted matcha and add a bit more beer. Whisk briefly. Add the rest of the beer.

ICED COLLAGEN MATCHA

Yield 1 serving

Sometimes we need an extra boost of protein.

- *1 cup hot water, 175 degrees F*
- *1 to 2 teaspoons matcha green tea powder*
- *2 tablespoons grass-fed collagen protein powder*

Blend the ingredients together and serve over ice.

SPICY MATCHA METABOLISM BOOSTER

Yield 1 serving

Add some spice to your life... and your metabolism.

- *juice of 1 to 2 citrus fruits of choice*
- *4 to 5 drops liquid vanilla stevia or a drizzle of grade B maple syrup*
- *1/4 teaspoon cayenne pepper*
- *1 cup water*
- *1 teaspoon matcha green tea powder*
- *1/8 teaspoon vanilla bean powder or a splash of vanilla extract*

Blend everything together and serve over ice.

A "HEALTHY" MATCHA GREEN SMOOTHIE

Yield 1 to 2 servings

Here's a great low-carb "healthy" green smoothie. The cucumber is hydrating; the celery has potassium; avocado has fat, folate, and vitamin E; lime has vitamin C and bioflavonoids; spinach has folate; ginger is anti-inflammatory; and broccoli sprouts bring serious anti-cancer nutrition.

- *1 cucumber, chopped*
- *1 celery stalk, chopped*
- *1 avocado, pitted and peeled*
- *10 leaves of fresh mint*
- *1/3 of a lime, with the peel*
- *1 pinch sea salt*
- *1 handful broccoli sprouts*
- *1 cup water*
- *1 knob fresh ginger, peeled*
- *1 handful spinach*
- *1/2 teaspoon matcha green tea powder*

Blend everything together and serve.

TROPICAL TURMERIC MATCHA SMOOTHIE

Yield 1 serving

This recipe was inspired by the beautiful island of Kauai. Let the tropical flavors take you there whenever you like.

- 1 1/2 to 2 cups water
- 1/2 teaspoon ground turmeric powder
- 1/4 cup dried coconut, shredded and unsweetened
- 1 cup frozen pineapple
- 1 cup frozen mango
- 1/2 teaspoon matcha green tea powder
- 1 tablespoon MCT oil

Blend everything until smooth.

CHOCOLATE MATCHA WORKOUT SHAKE

Yield 1 serving

A fun shake for after your next workout, with a bit of protein.

- *1 teaspoon matcha green tea powder*
- *2 tablespoons hemp seeds*
- *1 cup raw coconut water*
- *1 tablespoon cocoa powder*
- *1/4 to 1 teaspoon bee pollen*
- *ice*

Blend the matcha, hemp seeds, coconut water, cocoa, and bee pollen together. Serve over ice.

ICED LIME MATCHA REFRESHER

Yield 1 serving

This is refreshing on a hot summer day.

- *1 cup water*
- *1 teaspoon matcha green tea powder*
- *juice of 1 lime*

Blend everything together and pour over ice.

COCONUT WATER YOGA MATCHA

Yield 1 serving

I love raw coconut water and the matcha adds the perfect counterbalance to its sweetness. I am particularly fond of drinking this before a heated yoga class for hydration and to boost my concentration.

- *1 cup raw coconut water*
- *1/2 to 1 teaspoon matcha green tea powder*

Blend the ingredients and serve over ice.

MATCHA VANILLA BUTTER LATTE

Yield 1 serving

This recipe is one of my favorites, and I like it best slightly sweet via stevia. I make the drink at a lower temperature than the other recipes because I'm using essential oil and don't want to alter its nutrient value.

- 1 1/4 cups warm water, about 150 degrees F
- 1 tablespoon grass-fed (unsalted) butter, room temp
- 1/8 teaspoon vanilla bean powder
- 5 drops liquid vanilla stevia extract
- 2 drops ginger essential oil (or a knob of fresh ginger, chopped)
- 1 teaspoon matcha green tea powder

Blend everything together until smooth.

ZEN TONIC HERB MATCHA

Yield 1 serving

Tonic herbs have impressive health benefits. Adding them to a matcha tea drink makes a powerful combo.

- *3/4 cup hot water, 175 degrees F*
- *1 teaspoon cocoa powder*
- *1 teaspoon reishi powder (or a squirt of reishi tincture)*
- *1/2 teaspoon matcha green tea powder*
- *1 to 3 teaspoons freshly grated cacao butter*
- *sweetener, optional*

Blend everything together.

CREAMY COCONUT MATCHA

Yield 1 serving

I like a little coconut milk with my matcha. They work well together.

- *3/4 cup hot water, 175 degrees F*
- *1/2 teaspoon matcha green tea powder*
- *1/4 cup coconut milk*
- *2 drops liquid vanilla stevia*

Blend everything together.

BULLETPROOF™ MATCHA VANILLA BUTTER LATTE

Yield 1 serving

Dave Asprey created a life-changing recipe called Bulletproof Coffee™ when he blended coffee with grass-fed butter and his Brain Octane™ MCT oil* (an extra potent form of MCT oil). It's really good. In this recipe, I make it with matcha instead of coffee. It, too, is really good.

- 1 1/4 cups hot water, 175 degrees F
- 1 tablespoon grass-fed (unsalted) butter
- 1 tablespoon MCT oil
- 1 to 1 1/2 teaspoons matcha green tea powder
- 1/4 teaspoon vanilla bean powder

Blend all of the ingredients until smooth and creamy.

* Available at UpgradedSelf.com.

GRAPEFRUIT MATCHA CHIA FRESCA

Yield 1 serving

This is a wonderfully fresh, uplifting drink.

- *1 teaspoon chia seeds*
- *1 teaspoon matcha green tea powder*
- *1/2 cup water*
- *juice of 1 grapefruit*
- *freshly grated ginger (to taste)*
- *sweetener, if desired*

Place the chia seeds in a glass. Blend the rest of the ingredients and pour this mixture in the glass with chia seeds. Add ice. Stir and drink.

MEDITATION MATCHA

Yield 1 serving

Creamy, warm, and perfect for drinking before meditation.

- *1 tablespoon grated cacao butter*
- *1 tablespoon coconut butter*
- *1 1/2 teaspoons matcha green tea powder*
- *1 cup hot water, 175 degrees F*
- *4 to 5 drops vanilla liquid stevia*

Blend everything together until smooth and serve in your favorite mug.

WARMING MAGICAL MATCHA ELIXIR

Yield 1 serving

There are lots of goodies in this elixir to increase health, longevity, and brain power.

- *1 teaspoon matcha green tea powder*
- *2 teaspoons cocao powder*
- *1 cup hot water, 175 degrees F*
- *1 to 3 teaspoons MCT oil*
- *1 tablespoon grass-fed (unsalted) butter*
- *1/4 teaspoon ground turmeric powder*
- *2 to 3 grinds freshly ground black pepper*
- *1/8 teaspoon ground cinnamon powder*
- *cayenne powder or cayenne tincture, to taste*
- *sweetener, optional*

Blend everything together until smooth.

SPARKLING MATCHA WATER

Yield 1 serving

My family loves sparkling water. We call it "fizzy water." Adding matcha is fun and made it extra pretty.

- 1 to 1 1/2 cups sparkling mineral water
- 4 to 5 drops vanilla liquid stevia
- juice from 1/2 lime
- 1/2 tsp matcha green tea powder

Place the matcha, lime juice, and stevia in a glass with a few splashes of the sparkling water. Use a frother or whisk to mix. Add the rest of the sparkling mineral water and plenty of ice.

ROSE PETAL MATCHA ROMANCE TEA

Yield 1 serving

I am at a loss of words to describe the wonder of this combination. It's soft, delicate, and perfectly lovely.

- 1/2 cup water
- 1 tablespoon organic dried rose petals
- 1/2 teaspoon matcha green tea powder, sifted

Place the water and rose petals in a glass mason jar in the refrigerator overnight. The next day, strain the pretty pink rose tea into a small pan and warm to 175 degrees F. Transfer the tea to a cup with the sifted matcha in it. Froth or whisk the ingredients.

MATCHA CINNAMON BLEND

Yield 1 serving

Cinnamon and matcha are yummy together!

- 1 cup hot water, 175 degrees F
- 1/2 teaspoon ground cinnamon powder
- 1 teaspoon matcha green tea powder
- 1 tablespoon grass-fed (unsalted) butter
- 1 to 2 drops liquid hazelnut or vanilla stevia extract

Blend everything together.

UMEBOSHI GINGER MATCHA DIGESTION TEA

Yield 1 serving

Umeboshi plums are a popular, salty condiment in Japan. They are prized for longevity and helping digestion. If you're not used to umeboshi plums, I'll admit this tea is an acquired taste. However, it makes me feel so good when I drink it. I recommend you try it a few times before rendering an opinion.

- *1 cup spring water*
- *1 umeboshi plum, pitted*
- *1 knob of fresh ginger, grated*
- *1/2 teaspoon matcha green tea powder*

Heat the water, umeboshi plum, and ginger to a simmer for 2 to 3 minutes. Take off the heat and transfer to a blender. When the temperature cools to 175 degrees F, add the matcha and blend.

PART II
FOOD

MATCHA BUTTERED ORGANIC POPCORN

Yield 1 to 2 servings

I know a lot of people who love popcorn (hi, Mom!) and so I made this recipe for them. It's good!

- 4 tablespoons organic corn kernels
- 4 tablespoons melted grass-fed (salted) butter
- 1/2 teaspoon matcha green tea powder, sifted

Place the corn kernels in a brown paper bag and fold over the top of the bag two times. Place the bag, on its side, in a microwave oven and microwave it for about 2 minutes. You will hear a lot of popping of the popcorn, which is good, and as you hear the popping slow down, get ready to stop the microwave if necessary so that it does not over-cook.

While the popcorn is cooking in the microwave, warm your butter on the stove and whisk in the matcha. Transfer the popcorn from the bag to a large bowl, and pour the matcha butter on top. Toss to mix.

LUCKY MATCHA MASHED POTATOES

Yield 3 to 4 servings

These are fun mashed potatoes. Kids love 'em... *they're GREEN!*

- *2 russet potatoes, peeled*
- *sea salt and black pepper, to taste*
- *6 to 8 tablespoons grass-fed butter, room temperature*
- *1 teaspoon matcha, sifted*

Quarter the peeled potatoes and put in a medium pot filled with salted, cold water. Bring the water to a boil and cook until a knife easily pokes one (this could take 10 to 20 minutes).

While the potatoes are cooking, put the butter and matcha in a medium sized bowl. Take the potatoes out of the pot and add to the bowl with butter. Mash the potatoes with the butter and matcha. Season with plenty of sea salt and black pepper, to taste.

LADY BUGS ON A MOSSY LOG

Yield 1 serving

Like the old Ants on a Log recipe, but reimagined. Kids love it!

- *2 celery stalks*
- *2 tablespoons pumpkin seeds butter*
- *1/4 teaspoon matcha green tea powder, sifted*

- *1 pinch sea salt*
- *1 to 2 tablespoons goji berries*

In a small bowl, stir together the pumpkin seed butter, matcha, and salt. Spread the butter mixture onto the celery "logs" and top with "lady bug" goji berries.

MATCHA GRASS-FED BUTTER SPREAD

Yield 1 serving

Soft grass-fed butter and matcha are, well, cool. Spread this combo on crackers, organic sourdough toast, chocolate dipped rice cakes, and even a grass-fed burger.

- *1/4 teaspoon matcha green tea powder, sifted*
- *1 tablespoon grass-fed (salted) butter, room temperature*

Stir the ingredients together in a small bowl.

MATCHA MINI PESTO

Yield about 6 ounces

The best pestos are created without a set recipe... they just have lots of fresh herbs, sea salt, garlic, olive oil, and cheese (or hemp seeds in my case). Grab these ingredients for a small batch and make adjustments as you go to find your perfect creation. It'll be different every time.

- *1 handful fresh basil*
- *1 handful fresh mint leaves*
- *1 sprig fresh rosemary*

Matcha Mini Pesto

- 2 to 3 fresh sprigs fresh thyme
- 1 handful fresh cilantro or parsley
- 1 to 2 teaspoons matcha green tea powder
- 1/2 to 1 cup hemp seeds
- 1/4 to 1/2 teaspoon sea salt
- 2 cloves garlic, chopped
- olive oil

Place all of the ingredients in a food processor, fitted with the "S" blade, except for the olive oil. I use a mini-food processor for this. Start running the food processor to chop the ingredients and drizzle in the olive oil.

MATCHA SPICY TAHINI DRESSING (OR DIP)

Yield 1 cup

This light green dressing gives a decadence to salads and vegetables. Serve it as a salad dressing over raw bok choy or romaine lettuce. Or, use as a dip for vegetable crudité.

- *1/2 cup water, more as needed*
- *1/4 cup raw olive oil*
- *1/3 cup tahini*
- *3 tablespoons fresh lemon or lime juice*
- *1 teaspoon toasted sesame oil*
- *1/4 – 1/2 teaspoon cayenne pepper, to taste*
- *1/2 teaspoon sea salt*
- *1 teaspoon matcha green tea powder*

Blend all of the ingredients until smooth, adding more water as needed.

SWEET LEMON MATCHA SALAD DRESSING

Yield 1 cup

Great on salads and vegetables. This recipe is my mom's favorite.

- *1/2 cup raw olive oil*
- *2 tablespoons raw honey*
- *2 tablespoons apple cider vinegar*
- *zest of 1 organic lemon*
- *6 tablespoons fresh organic lemon juice*

- *1 teaspoon sea salt*
- *1/2 teaspoon matcha*
- *1/4 teaspoon black pepper*

Blend everything and serve on salad. Store leftover dressing in the refrigerator.

MAPLE MATCHA GUMMIES

Yield 10 to 20 servings (depending on size)

- *1 1/2 cups water (or herbal tea), room temperature*
- *2 tablespoons grass-fed collagen gelatin powder**
- *1 teaspoon matcha green tea powder*
- *2 to 4 tablespoons grade B maple syrup*

In a small pan, add the ingredients and whisk to incorporate. Use low heat to heat just slightly, until gelatin is dissolved (about 5 minutes or less), whisking as needed during this time. Pour the mixture into a shallow glass baking dish (or silicone molds), and refrigerate for a few hours. Cut into squares.

* I use Collagelatin from UpgradedSelf.com

MATCHA BREAKFAST ENERGY YOGURT

Yield 1 serving

This is one of my daughter's favorite breakfasts. "Extra raisins, please," she says.

- *6 to 8 tablespoons whole-fat, grass-fed Greek yogurt*
- *1/2 teaspoon matcha green tea powder, sifted*
- *2 tablespoons raisins or goji berries*

Place the yogurt in a bowl. Stir the sifted matcha into it and add raisins or goji berries.

SOFTLY SCRAMBLED MATCHA EGGS

Yield 1 serving

Dr. Seuss ain't got nothin' on these green eggs. We're big egg eaters in our house and adding matcha to them is fun. For extra Dr. Seussness, add ham.

- *2 pasture-raised organic eggs*
- *1 pinch sea salt*
- *1/2 teaspoon matcha green tea powder, sifted*

Whisk together the eggs, salt and matcha. Scramble them gently over low heat.

MATCHA CARDAMOM GLUTEN-FREE BLENDER PANCAKES

Yield 3 to 4 pancakes

I like blender pancakes because blending everything just makes it easier.

- *1 banana, peeled*
- *2 eggs*
- *1/4 teaspoon vanilla bean powder*
- *1/2 teaspoon ground cardamom powder*
- *1/2 teaspoon ground turmeric powder*
- *1 tablespoon flax seeds, ground*
- *1 tablespoon coconut flour*
- *1 pinch sea salt*
- *1 fresh grind of black pepper*
- *1 1/2 teaspoons matcha green tea powder*
- *ghee, for cooking*

Blend the ingredients together. Wait a few minutes for the batter to thicken. Heat a bit of ghee in a pan over medium heat.

Pour some pancake batter into the heated skillet. Let the pancake cook for a couple of minutes, depending on the level of heat you use. Flip the pancake and cook a bit more.

APPLE PEAR MATCHA "PORRIDGE"

Yield 1 serving

A lightly sweet and quick "porridge" made in the blender.

- 1/4 cup almond milk*
- 1 green or red pear, cored and chopped
- 1 red or green apple, cored and chopped
- 2 teaspoons raw honey or maple syrup
- 1/4 teaspoon ground allspice powder (or chinese 5-spice)
- 1/4 teaspoon matcha green tea powder

Put the ingredients in a blender and briefly puree.

* I like to make my own fresh raw almond milk.

MATCHA BANANA MASH

Yield 1 serving

This is a quick breakfast or snack option when you need a bit of energy and have a hankering for a bit of sweetness. It's a kid-pleaser, too!

- *1 ripe banana, peeled and chopped*

- *1/4 teaspoon matcha green tea powder, sifted*
- *1 teaspoon grated raw cacao butter*
- *granola or chopped nuts for texture*

Stir everything together in a small bowl.

MATCHA WHIPPED CREAM

Yield about 2 cups

I prefer a lot of things unsweetened for health reasons and so I make my whipped cream without sweetener. Feel free to sweeten it up though! Serve this cool whipped cream on top of coffee, matcha tea, ice cream, chocolate brownies, or whatever needs a delicious dollop of whipped cream.

- *2 cups cold grass-fed whipping cream**
- *1 tablespoon matcha green tea powder*
- *sweetener, if desired*

Blend the ingredients in a high-speed blender until whipped (about 20 to 25 seconds).

* I buy Straus grass-fed whipping cream at Whole Foods Market.

MATCHA ENERGY NUT BUTTER

Yield 1 cup

My daughter and husband like this spread in celery for an afternoon snack.

- *1/2 cup natural organic peanut butter or almond butter*
- *1/2 cup dried coconut, shredded and unsweetened*
- *1/4 cup raw Brazil nut butter*

- *1 tablespoon raw honey*
- *3 tablespoons dark chocolate chips*
- *1 1/2 to 2 teaspoons matcha green tea powder*
- *1 pinch sea salt*

Stir everything together in a bowl and transfer to a glass jar with a lid.

This can be used to make a Matcha Energy Nut Milk by blending 1 to 2 tablespoons with a cup of water.

MATCHA-DUSTED, GARLIC-BUTTERED MOCHI

Yield 4 to 12, depending on how many you make

Mochi is a fun and chewy pillow of goodness to eat. We load them up with grass-fed butter for extra nutrition. When matcha entered our life... well, we added that to them, too.

- *mochi**
- *grass-fed (salted) butter, softened or melted*
- *matcha green tea powder, sifted*

Bake the mochi per the instructions on the package, as many as you desire. Pour (or spread) salted butter on top and finish with sifted matcha.

* I buy mochi in the refrigerated section of Whole Foods Market.

MATCHA GUACAMOLE

Yield 3 to 4 servings

Pair with organic corn chips, crackers, sourdough toast, or veggies and enjoy.

- *2 to 3 ripe avocados, pitted and peeled*
- *1 drizzle raw olive oil*
- *1 squeeze fresh lime juice (or splash of apple cider vinegar)*
- *sea salt, to taste*

- *3/4 teaspoon matcha green tea powder, sifted*
- *1/4 teaspoon garlic powder*
- *1 handful fresh cilantro, chopped*
- *1/8 teaspoon ground coriander powder*
- *freshly ground black pepper, to taste*

Mash everything together in a bowl.

MATCHA TUNA SALAD

Yield 1 serving

Adding matcha to my tuna salad was a no-brainer, as it adds a hint of vegetal flavoring and nutrition.

If you're making this recipe for more than one person, double or triple it.

- *1 can tuna**
- *2 to 3 tablespoons grass-fed, full-fat yogurt***
- *1 pitted prune, diced*
- *1/2 stalk celery, minced*
- *1 teaspoon diced leek or onion*
- *1 squeeze fresh lemon juice*
- *1/4 teaspoon dried dill*
- *1/4 teaspoon matcha green tea powder, sifted*

Place all of the ingredients, except for the matcha, in a medium sized bowl. Stir together briefly to mix. Add the sifted matcha and stir to combine. Serve.

* If you consume tuna frequently, tuna is a concern. I prefer Wild Planet tuna, which can be found on Amazon.com and at some Costco stores. Wild Planet catches only small tuna, which makes for a lower mercury content. Check out their website for more information: WildPlanetFoods.com.

** My favorite brand for whole-fat, grass-fed Greek yogurt is Straus, which I buy at Whole Foods Market.

MATCHA ICE CUBES

Yield 1 ice cube tray's worth

Ice cubes made with matcha tea look so cool.

- *1 cup water*
- *1 teaspoon matcha green tea powder*

Blend the water and matcha. Pour into an ice cube tray and freeze.

Transfer the frozen cubes to a bag or glass jar for storage in the freezer. Make another batch so you have plenty on hand. Serve some of the cubes in your next iced beverage for a groovy-looking matcha boost.

ALMOND ALLSPICE MATCHA CHIA PUDDING

Yield 1 to 2 servings

Chia puddings are so fun! Try different spices and nut butters to create variety. These are perfect for breakfasts and snacks.

- *4 tablespoons chia seeds*
- *1/2 teaspoon ground allspice, freshly ground if possible*
- *1 teaspoon matcha green tea powder*
- *1 cup water*
- *3 tablespoons almond butter, or any nut or seed butter*
- *3 to 5 drops liquid vanilla stevia extract*

Place the chia seeds in a pint glass mason jar. Blend the remaining ingredients together and pour into the jar. Put on a lid and shake it well. Wait a few minutes and shake again. Repeat. Store in the refrigerator at least 4 hours to firm.

LEMON MATCHA CHOCOLATE PUDDING

4 servings

Making chocolate pudding with avocado is something I've done for years. Adding matcha is new and exciting.

- 1/4 cup fresh lemon juice
- zest of 1 small lemon
- 2 medium avocados, peeled and pitted
- 2 tablespoons grass-fed (unsalted) butter, softened
- 1 1/2 teaspoons matcha green tea powder
- 1/4 cup cocoa powder
- 6 tablespoons maple syrup
- 1 pinch sea salt

Blend everything together and serve immediately or chill prior to serving.

MATCHA BREAKFAST COCONUT ICE CREAM (LOW-CARB)

Yield 1 pint

Sometimes I blend a scoop of this into my coffee in the morning. Other times I have it in place of coffee.

- *6 raw pasture-raised egg yolks*
- *2 tablespoons MCT oil*

Matcha Breakfast Coconut Ice Cream (Low-Carb)

- 1/4 teaspoon vanilla bean powder
- 6 tablespoons grass-fed (unsalted) butter, softened
- 6 tablespoons coconut oil
- 1 tablespoon matcha green tea powder
- 1/4 cup USA non-GMO birchwood xylitol
- 1/2 cup water
- 1 pinch sea salt

Blend everything together and transfer to an ice cream maker. Follow the manufacturer's instructions.

SWEET MATCHA BARS

Yield 1 (8x8) glass-baking dish

The first time I made these, I was giddy by the flavors and how pretty they turned out. Make this for your dish to pass the next time you go to a party. You'll get invited back again.

Filling Ingredients

- 20 prunes, pitted
- 5 medjool dates, pitted
- 2 teaspoons matcha green tea powder
- 1 teaspoon ground cinnamon powder
- 1/2 teaspoon vanilla bean powder
- water

Crumble Ingredients

- 1 cup almonds
- 1 cup cashews
- 3 tablespoons USA non-GMO birchwood xylitol or unrefined cane sugar
- 2 tablespoons MCT oil or coconut oil
- 2 teaspoons matcha green tea powder
- 2 pinches sea salt

Filling Instructions

Place the pitted dates and prunes in a bowl with the matcha, cinnamon, and vanilla. Add just enough spring water to be just under the dried fruit. Let them soak for about a half hour and then blend everything, adding a little more water as needed for a thick puree. Set aside in a bowl while you make the crumble.

Crumble Instructions

Place all of the crumble ingredients in a food processor, fitted with the "S" blade, and process until it starts to stick together a bit when pressed gently between two of your fingers.

Assembly Instructions

Take a little more than half of the crumble mixture and press it firmly into the bottom of an 8x8 glass baking dish. Spread the prune filling on top. Then, sprinkle the remaining crumble on top of the date filling, and gently press down.

If desired, put the dessert in the oven to warm a bit.

SIMPLE BROCCOLI MATCHA SOUP

Yield 2 servings

This can be made the night before and warmed gently the next morning for breakfast. Or make it as an energizing, pick-me-up lunch.

- 2 cups hot bone broth, 175 degrees F
- 1 bunch organic broccoli florets, steamed lightly
- 2 tablespoons grass-fed (salted) butter
- sea salt and black pepper
- 1 tablespoon matcha green tea powder
- 1 squeeze fresh lemon juice

Blend everything together. Season with sea salt as needed.

CHILLED MATCHA BEAUTY SOUP

Yield 2 servings

Here is a soup that does everything to support you being your most radiant.

- 1 organic cucumber, chopped
- 1 avocado, pitted and peeled
- 1 green onion, chopped
- 4 large fresh basil leaves
- 1 squeeze fresh organic lime juice
- 1/2 cup plain, full-fat grass-fed yogurt
- 1 cup raw coconut water
- 1 sprig fresh dill
- 2 teaspoons fresh aloe meat
- 1 teaspoon matcha
- 1/4 teaspoon sea salt, more to taste

Blend everything together until smooth.

MATCHA MISO SOUP

Yield 1 serving

Miso soup makes a fast and nourishing breakfast. Adding matcha is the perfect hack for infusing it with some caffeine.

- *1 cup hot water, 175 degrees F*
- *1 teaspoon matcha green tea powder, sifted*
- *1 to 3 teaspoons non-GMO miso*

Whisk together the warm water and the matcha. Let it cool to about 130 degrees F and stir in the miso. For an extra dose of probiotics, serve with a side of kimchi.

COCONUT MINT CHIP MATCHA ICE CREAM

Yield a little over 1 pint

Mint chocolate chip has always been my favorite ice cream so it was only natural that I made one with matcha, which naturally turned it green.

- *1 1/2 cups coconut milk*
- *1/2 cup water*
- *4 tablespoons grass-fed (unsalted) butter, room temperature*
- *1 teaspoon peppermint extract*
- *10 fresh mint leaves*
- *1 tablespoon matcha green tea powder*
- *6 tablespoons USA non-GMO birchwood xylitol*
- *1/4 cup dark chocolate chips*

Blend everything together, except for the chocolate chips. Add the chocolate chips and blend briefly. Pour the mixture into an ice cream maker and follow the manufacturer's instructions for use.

PART III
FACIAL MASKS

MATCHA BEAUTY MASK

Yield 1 face mask

Clay masks are great for detoxifying and clearing the skin. The epigalloticechin gallate (EGCG) in matcha is helpful for reducing inflammation and balancing skin tone.

- *1 tablespoon clay mask**
- *1/4 teaspoon matcha green tea powder, sifted*
- *1 drop lavender or tea tree essential oil, if desired*

- *1 to 2 tablespoons, more or less as needed, liquid of choice (citrus juice, spring water, raw honey, yogurt, hydrosol)*

Mix everything in a glass bowl with a plastic or wooden spoon (glass, plastic, and wood are non-reactive). Apply on face and wait 10 to 20 minutes before gently rinsing it off.

* I buy Alitura face mask, available online.

MATCHA 'N' ALOE HEALING SKIN MASK

Yield 1 face mask

Combining matcha with aloe's benefits makes this a great mask for healing skin.

- *1 aloe leaf, filleted*
- *1/4 teaspoon matcha green tea powder, sifted*

Mix the ingredients together in a bowl and put on your face for 10 to 20 min. Gently rinse off.

CONCLUSION

Matcha is a great addition to your life. It can give you the perfect boost of energy mid-day, enhance your immune system during the holidays and times of travel or stress, supercharge your brain's focus, and it tastes great. With the recipes in this book, you'll be able to experience these health benefits multiple times a day.

I hope you've found this book to be helpful and that you add lots of matcha to your life!

Did you enjoy this book?

If so, please leave a review at Amazon!

As an independent author, your reviews are extremely helpful in getting the word out. After you leave a review, please drop me a line at kristen@HappySexyMillionaire.me so I can thank you!

Kristen's blog: HappySexyMillionaire.me

Twitter: @KristensRaw

Instagram: Kristen_Helmstetter

Made in United States
Troutdale, OR
12/01/2024

25592815R00056